Contents

Introduction

The eighties, like all other decades, had its problems. When the human race is given free rein over the planet, they are bound to make mistakes along the way, some larger and more devastating than others. Strangely, it is the so-called 'regular' folk who get us through these times after the powers-that-be mess up.

It is the person on the street who smiles in the face of adversity, and it is your local butcher who cracks a joke whenever you pop in for a rack of lamb. It is the eccentric kid at school who makes the class smile when there is some shocking news on the TV that morning. And it is the caring doctors and nurses at our local hospital working extortionately long hours to bandage us up when we've had a spill.

Anyone who lived through the eighties is a part of it and the allure it still possesses. No one person is more important than the other in making it what it was, and like the mechanism inside an antique watch, each of the little cogs moves another, creating the friction needed to push the decade along.

The eighties seemed to move especially fast, and technological breakthroughs in home entertainment, movies, and music seemed to be a daily occurrence. Compact Discs were replacing vinyl and cassettes, home video was part of life, and going to the cinema meant seeing cartoons meshing with live action in a seamless display of aesthetical wonder.

Toys were never cooler, and we were given the Care Bears, Strawberry Shortcake, the Pogo Ball, Teenage Mutant Ninja Turtles, the Rubik's Cube, Speak and Spell, and the oh-so-frustrating yet addictive Simon. The life of a child in the eighties was one of wonder, with everything advertised on TV a must-have. It was magical.

Of course, there were horror stories too, and as fabulous as the people on this planet can be, there will always be those who only want to cause pain and misery. Even as the memory of the incarcerated Yorkshire Ripper was still fresh, another gruesome discovery in Muswell Hill would stir it all up again and have the British public double-locking their doors.

Chernobyl reminded people that nuclear disaster was only one flawed reactor away, and the fear surrounding the AIDS epidemic was palpable. Football saw more disasters in one decade than it had known since its creation, and crack was covering most of America in a white blanket of anger and desperation. The miners' strikes nearly brought Britain to its knees, and the race riots and unemployment was like nothing ever seen before or since.

Throughout it all, art and expression continued to

flow. People found a way to enjoy themselves despite it all, and for those who lived in the eighties, they will generally only have fond memories when they reminisce. The clothes were glittery and flamboyant, and the TV shows were over-the-top and outrageous. Hair was permed—for both men and women—and shoulder pads in the ladies' dresses made them look like comical linebackers. But it was all in good fun, and the eighties proved that no matter what the dark part of the world throws at the bright side, it will never make us cower.

1980: Football Hooliganism and Lennon Passes

In the seventies, the music scene had been dominated by the invasion of punk. The Sex Pistols had somehow climbed out of the shadows of their more pop-inclined peers with their middle finger pointed directly at capitalism, and it had seemed like revolution was in the air. Despite the roadblocks put in front of them and their counterparts, the punk rock star shone brightly for a few angsty years. As the people were calling the seventies a day, the Bee Gees, Michael Jackson, disco, and funk were taking the charts by storm. People wanted bright colours, outrageous clothes, cocaine, digital advances, and bad haircuts. The eighties gladly provided.

When we think of the eighties, it is hard to do so without being drawn to Britain. As America was becoming a place for huge advertisement campaigns, sugary treats, fast food, blockbuster movies, and fast living, the British Isles were in turmoil. The Irish Republican Army (IRA) seemed to be detonating bombs on a weekly basis, unemployment hit a post-World War I high, and the Iron Lady threw a sour scowl over the masses and told them to follow her ideals or be left behind.

By 1980, one year after Margaret Thatcher was named Prime Minister, the UK had 1,600,000 people unemployed. On the streets, tensions were reaching boiling point, and riots in London and all over Britain were starting to become commonplace. This anger and hatred spilled into the country's football grounds, and the hooliganism that had really kicked off in the previous decade would go on to unimaginable levels in the eighties.

The Prime Minister's stance was made clear in October of 1981 when she gave her now infamous "This lady's not for turning" speech, in which she demanded the people of Britain maintain with her until they came to a "winter of common sense." Such words were meant to inspire, but when faced with another week on the dole, the majority of unemployed Britons would have felt that words were cheap.

Mixed in with all of the people's financial worries was the ever-present fear that had been cast over Leeds, Sheffield, and Bradford—and the whole of England—by the seemingly endless murders being committed by the Yorkshire Ripper. His reign of terror had been years-long by 1980, and the already ridiculed police force was in danger of becoming a laughingstock. In September, another woman would be attacked on the streets of Leeds on her way home. She would somehow survive the brutality, but with severe injuries and the long-term trauma caused by such an event, it would be devastating. By now, women throughout the nation were afraid to leave their homes after dark.

Given the drastic unemployment numbers in Britain, the news that the sixpence would be soon phased out seemed to feel like some sort of tragic irony. With penny-pinching now a way of life for the struggling country, losing the currency so synonymous with a Britain now gone would have felt very apt. It seemed that the younger generation who had been so vocal in the previous decade had only gone and freed themselves from everything but financial security.

In music, the world lost the first of two legends in May of 1980 when Joy Division vocalist and main songwriter Ian Curtis hanged himself in his Macclesfield home one day before the band was about to begin their U.S. tour. Curtis had long suffered from depression and epilepsy, both of which were handled with the "just have another drink and you'll be fine" method so akin to musicians at the time. Getting help with mental health issues—especially in men—was a long way away from anything even bordering on competence, and the world mourned a man who had possessed the potential to change the way we view lyrics in modern music.

Of course, the biggest shock, maybe in music history, was the cold-blooded murder of Beatles legend and peace activist John Lennon. The genius, who had been in the process of recording a new album with his wife, Yoko Ono, in New York, was shot several times by Mark Chapman outside his apartment building. Lennon would be proclaimed dead in a local hospital not long after, and the shockwaves felt around the world would be palpable.

His song, "(Just Like) Starting Over," which had been set for release around the time of his death, went straight to number one in America, Britain, and most of the world. Many posthumous releases would follow through the years, and Lennon's influence on music would be infinite. It is hard to imagine a time when he won't be seen as the most iconic musician that ever lived, and the mindless reasons for his far-too-soon passing will never be comprehensible to anyone but the lunatic who pulled the trigger.

In Washington State, Mount St. Helens erupted on May 18, causing devastation and panic in the state and in the surrounding area. Following an earthquake that erupted below the mountain, the largest landslide in recorded history followed, and scattered ash was seen in the skies in a twelve-state radius. The sound of the blast was recorded to have been heard up to 300 miles away, and it was so powerful that it removed 1,300 feet off the summit. In the aftermath, it would be discovered that 57 people lost their lives.

Another disaster, this one triggered by an electrical fault, saw the MGM Grand in Las Vegas engulfed in the deadliest fire in Nevada history. Caused by a poorly installed pastry display unit, the fire spread rapidly, trapping many people on the higher floors.

The whole casino and hotel were found to be well below code, and the aftermath saw newer, more stringent laws introduced in both building codes and the Life Safety Code. With 85 casualties, some would say that these changes came a little too late, and three months later, the Las Vegas Hilton would suffer the same fate, with eight casualties as a result. It seemed that the new codes and laws were being poorly implemented.

In sports, Americans were treated to one of the most iconic moments of all time. The Winter Olympics, which were being held in Lake Placid, New York, was set to be dominated by the Soviets. With the Cold War still raging and the obvious rivalry between the US and the USSR, tensions reached fever pitch when the two nations were drawn against each other in the medal round of the men's ice hockey tournament.

The USSR had won gold in five out of the previous six games, and they were odds on favourites to do so again. The Soviet team was made up of full international and professional hockey players, whereas the US was composed mostly of amateurs. With the Soviets leading 3 to 2 going into the final third, things looked bleak for the States. But midway through the last period, the US somehow scored twice, prompting commentator Al Michaels to proclaim, "Do you believe in miracles? Yes!" With this, The Miracle on Ice was born.

In the NBA, the 1979/80 season saw rookie Earvin Johnson move to the LA Lakers as the first draft pick. The man (who would soon be known the world over as Magic Johnson) admitted that he had picked the Lakers over every other franchise because of Kareem Abdul-Jabbar, LA's 7-foot 2-inch center, who had already become one of the hottest properties in basketball.

Despite Abdul-Jabbar regularly totting up more points than any other player in the NBA, he was yet to win a championship. That all would change with the signing of Magic when they won it in the first season of the two playing together, and the Lakers would go on to have one of the fiercest back-and-forth rivalries in NBA history throughout the eighties as they battled with the Boston Celtics. In the draft the previous season, the Celtics had signed their own soon-to-be legend when they snapped up Larry Bird.

Back in England, the country continued in vain to cope with the continuing rise in football hooliganism. Even with the constant violence regularly making the front pages, the actual football still produced some wonderful back page stories. Brian Clough's astonishing revolution at Nottingham Forest continued when his side retained the European Cup, becoming the first British club in history to have won more continental honours than domestic league titles.

Bob Paisley's Liverpool retained their league championship, while Arsenal were shocked in the FA Cup final by a gutsy Second Division West Ham when they were beaten by their London rivals one goal to nil at Wembley. Arsenal would compound a disappointing season by losing on penalties to Valencia in the European Cup Winners' Cup final.

In Hollywood, the era of the blockbuster continued on from the seventies, and Star Wars: The Empire Strikes Back—the sequel to the record-breaking Star Wars—inevitably cleaned up at the box office, raking in almost double that of its second-place competitor, 9 to 5. Although Star Wars began a massive trend in movies being profitably released alongside toys and merchandise, the eighties also saw a growing demand for films that would make them laugh, proven by the fact that seven of the top 10 highest-grossing movies in American cinema that year were comedies, including the timeless Airplane and the wonderful Richard Prior and Gene Wilder effort, Stir Crazy.

Among the undeniable glamour of the decade, with colourful clothes, makeup, roller skates, big-budget movies, disco music, and the launch of Post-it notes, the eighties had a dark undercurrent running through it. Things in the Western World looked bleak, and it felt like mindless violence was becoming the norm. Instead of fighting for a cause as the younger generation had done in the fifties and sixties, it seemed now that the kids were just fighting for the hell of it.

Tragedies like the senseless murder of John Lennon and the tragic suicide of Ian Curtis only added to the rage, as people started to feel that even the greats had had enough. Almost like fate was trying to turn up the heat, America also experienced one of its worst-ever heatwaves in the summer of 1980, as the Midwestern States were exposed to brutal temperatures that brought massive drought and caused some of the most devastating natural disasters in recent history. The damage caused to agriculture is estimated at 20 billion dollars in today's market, and 1,117 people lost their lives.

In Britain, the riots and hooliganism that had seemed so rife already were only going to worsen as the decade progressed, and with the IRA stepping up their terror campaign, Margaret Thatcher's job looked impossible. On top of that, the Yorkshire Ripper was still on the loose, and any faith the public had in those that made the decisions was running on fumes. Violence was everywhere, and the people of Britain and the rest of the world were becoming afraid. It would take one almighty coming together to make it out the other side.

1981: Riots and Unemployment

On January 2, 1981, Peter Sutcliffe, known to the media and the millions he terrified as the Yorkshire Ripper, was stopped by police in Sheffield as he parked in the driveway of the Light Trades House on Melbourne Avenue. Sutcliffe had a 24-year-old prostitute, Olivia Reivers, in his car, and when constable Robert Hayes decided to check the license plates, he discovered they were fake. When he told Peter Sutcliffe to accompany him to the station, he agreed but asked if he could urinate first in the alleyway close by, to which the police officer agreed.

Later on, when Sutcliffe's behavior at the station caused suspicion, the arresting officer returned to the scene and checked the alleyway, where they found a hammer, knife, and a rope that had been stashed behind a dumpster. Later, they would also discover another knife in a toilet cistern back at the station. After two days of intensive questioning, Peter Sutcliffe admitted to being the Yorkshire Ripper and soon went into a long, drawn-out confession, proclaiming several more murders than had been originally suspected.

Sutcliffe was officially charged on January 5th with 13 counts of murder, and a nation that had been under so much stress breathed a sigh of relief. His subsequent trial later in the year would bring massive worldwide media coverage, and the images of the public spitting at the police van outside the courthouse and hurling vehement abuse will forever be etched in the memory of anyone who has seen it. Although the Ripper was caught, there was a long way—and endless emotional pain—still to go in the whole process.

Falling in line with the media hype surrounding the arrest of Sutcliffe, controversial and unpopular media tycoon Rupert Murdoch continued his ever-growing monopoly of media outlets across Britain, Australia, and the US. His news outlets, such as FOX, News of the World, and The Sun newspaper, would make the lives of celebrities and anyone considered newsworthy a living hell for decades to come. Murdoch, who would be known for hiring only the sleaziest of journalists, proved that there would be no depths his outlets and employees wouldn't sink to get a scoop, including the disgusting phone-hacking revelations about his company, News Corporation, in July 2001.

His business model of shock, controversy, scandal, and outright lies—if the news day were slow—would be the beginning of the end for anything ever bordering on credible journalism. From the moment he started buying up as many media outlets as possible, the tabloid newspapers overtook the broadsheets in sales, and suddenly bare-breasted women on page three replaced well-written political satire and researched journalism. What was once an honourable profession was now nothing more than scouring through a pop singer's trash.

Prince Charles and Lady Diana Spencer announced their engagement in February after six months of dating. Diana, who was 19 at the time, looked awkward and uncomfortable in a joint interview at Buckingham Palace, broadcast live on BBC. Thirty-two-year-old Charles told the nation that he was "delighted" and "frankly amazed that Diana would take him on." When asked if the couple were in love, Charles gave an answer Diana would admit years later had traumatized her when he meekly said, "Whatever love means" (Jessen, 2022. para 4).

We know now that the marriage was doomed, and through it all, Lady Di would become not only Britain's sweetheart but that of the world. At a time when the monarchy's influence was waning for the first time, the engagement of the two royals—however awkward and staged as it seems in hindsight—lifted the nation's spirits a little, regardless. It seemed that even though Britain was in the midst of an unemployment pandemic and the streets were filled with rage, the general public still loved a nice royal showpiece.

Among the many riots breaking out all over England —both racially motivated and aimed at the unemployment numbers—two of the most severe that year happened in Brixton, London, and

Toxteth, Liverpool. In Brixton, tensions between police and the black community spilled over when the death of a local man saw police brutality called into question. The destruction that followed caused over £8 million ($10 million US) worth of damage, and 365 police and civilians were injured.

In Liverpool, the arrest of a local black man who claimed he was mistreated at the police station caused nine days of rioting. Petrol bombs and paving stones were thrown at the riot police, and several vehicles were set alight. The Merseyside police were not fully trained for such heavy aggression on as large a scale, and the flimsy shields they were provided did little to stop the scaffolding poles and petrol bombs being used against them.

Amidst all the racial tension, IRA martyr Bobby Sands died in prison on May 5th after a 66-day hunger strike. His passing would cause even more riots to break out, this time in Belfast, and throughout the year, six more of his fellow IRA members and three of the Irish Liberation Army would pass away. Before his death, Sands had been elected to an empty seat in the British Parliament, but he would never get to use it. His funeral saw more than 100,000 people attend, and in October, Margaret Thatcher agreed to a few of the protestors' demands, including visits and the right to receive mail, bringing an end to the strike.

The AIDS crisis, which had begun to spread fear through America, showed up in Britain in 1981 when the first case was diagnosed in December. Disgustingly, it was still being reported as a "gay disease," causing millions of heterosexual men and women to continue having unprotected sex. The blind bigotry of a few higher-ups and the media would be the cause of an endless number of avoidable deaths in the years to follow.

In America, the style-over-substance lifestyle was in full flow. New money, appearance, expensive drugs, and digital gimmicks were all the rage. This was most notably epitomized with the introduction of the DeLorean car. The silver exterior and gull-wing doors were just the ticket for the fast-paced, high-living movers and shakers who couldn't quite afford a real, bona fide sports car. The car itself, which was already being reported to suffer from severe issues, such as horrible driving experience and poor structure, sold quite well early on, but it didn't last. Even today, when it still maintains its full-time place on anyone's Top 10 List of Woeful Automobiles, its popularity remains, mainly down to its usage in the Back to the Future trilogy.

In August of 1981, a product released by IBM would change the face of modern technology as we know it. The introduction of the world's first affordable PC had 10 times the memory capacity of any other machine on the market and was much faster too. Its sleek design was appealing to the masses also, and having one on a desk in your New York apartment was the dream of millions of twenty-somethings at the time. If your desk sat by a window that looked out over your shiny new DeLorean, then you'd really made it.

With the Space Race dying out ever since Neil Armstrong walked on the moon in 1969, NASA still continued to explore the great unknown. Their first-ever space shuttle launch in August still caught the people's imagination, but nothing like it had two decades before. The idea of the mission was to successfully send a shuttle into space, then manage to return it to Earth in such a condition that it could be used again. Three workers were killed and five injured in a failed test launch a month before its maiden voyage. Although still considered a successful endeavor once the actual mission was completed, America was starting to wonder why the billions being spent on the space program weren't being put to more practical use.

Super Bowl XV produced a shock when the Oakland Raiders became the first-ever wildcard playoff team to win the championship. The game took place at the Louisiana Superdome in New Orleans, but the pre-game ceremonies were overshadowed by the recent ending of the Iran hostage crisis, with most of the crowd seeming angry and agitated. On the field, two touchdown passes from quarterback Jim Plunkett gave the Raiders a 14-0 lead in the opening quarter, which they never let go, running out 27-10 winners in the end.

The NBA season was another monumental effort, and the pendulum between the Lakers and the Celtics swung again, with Boston winning their first championship since 1976. Larry Bird, who was already becoming a fan favourite, was joined by the signings of Kevin McHale and Robert Parish, and The Big Three was born. The Celtics overcame the Houston Rockets by four games to two in a final that was befitting of the season that had preceded it. The NBA in the eighties was clearly in its zenith.

Back in Britain, the English clubs continued their astonishing domination of European football when Liverpool beat the mighty Real Madrid 1-0 in the final to lift the European Cup, thus keeping the trophy on English soil for the fifth year running. More impressively, up-and-coming managerial genius Bobby Robson guided minnows Ipswich to the UEFA Cup final, where they beat Dutch side AZ Alkmaar 5-4 on aggregate to win their first and only European title.

Bobby Robson and his Ipswich side were also holding their own in the domestic league, and in a championship race that went right to the wire, they only narrowly lost out to a plucky Aston Villa side, who claimed their first league title since 1910. The mighty Liverpool finished in a lowly fifth position, but the joy of winning the European Cup saved their blushes. Throughout all of this, one of the world's most famous clubs, Manchester United, had a horrendous campaign, finishing in eighth place. This would cost manager Dave Sexton his job. He would be replaced by the charismatic Ron Atkinson.

Hooliganism continued to be a growing problem in Britain, and unemployment had jumped to a staggering 2,400,000. Tensions continued to rise, and the public was not content with the crumbs being afforded them from the politicians' table. Margaret Thatcher continued to tell the people of Britain to trust her process, but her voice seemed to be getting drowned out by the yells of rioters and the bombs of the Irish Republican Army.

America saw some change when Ronald Reagan became their 40th president, and along with his second in command, George W. Bush, they began their campaign by announcing the release of the 52 Americans that had been held in captivity in Iran for 444 days minutes after their inauguration, effectively ending the Iranian hostage situation. In July, President Reagan announced the promotion of Sandra Day O'Connor to the Supreme Court of the United States, making her the first female to be given such an honour.

The eighties were a time in America when it seemed like every significant 'first' was occurring there. Even with the crime rate growing, the glamour and stardust associated with the US continued to shine, and the rest of the world looked on in wonder as each new movie painted a picture of a country where the soft drinks were sweeter, the people more beautiful, and the TV screens larger. This yearning for American culture was never more evident than with the launch of MTV in August of 1981, and it seemed that for the first time in history, TV channels and media outlets were being aimed at the youth.

By 1981, everything seemed to have been sped up drastically, and catching your breath was nearly impossible to do. Just as people adjusted to some new digital advance or advertising gimmick, they were slapped in the face with another, more advanced one. Movie posters now adorned the kids' walls alongside musicians and sporting icons, and the rest of the planet struggled to hold onto their identity as a desperate need for Americanization spread through the youth.

1982: Madonna and Maradona

The entertainment world continued to explode in 1982, and in music, the world was blown away by the release of Michael Jackson's Thriller. It would be Jackson's sixth studio album and the first to go to number one, where it stayed for a record-breaking 37 weeks. Produced by the legendary Quincy Jones, the album was a step away from disco for Jackson, with the genre that had taken the late seventies by storm being accused by the music industry and the public as being cheap, tacky, and repetitive.

Astonishingly, Thriller would be so stacked with hits that the record company released seven singles off it, including "Billie Jean," "Wanna Be Startin' Somethin'," "The Girl Is Mine," and, of course, the title track, "Thriller." The latter would also bring about the first real foray by a pop star into the mostly untapped music video world. Although music videos had been made before, nobody had put much effort in. With Jackson's zombie-influenced masterpiece, all that changed, with kids across America sitting by their television for hours on end, just waiting for the next showing of "Thriller" on the newly launched MTV.

This was the year that also gave the world their first glimpse of a young pop star by the name of

Madonna. Her debut single "Everybody" and the accompanying low-budget music video of her dancing in the club with her friends paved the way for her journey to the top. The single, released in early October, was followed by her debut album in '83, which would stay on the pop charts for over a year and spawn the timeless single, "Holiday." Within three years, Madonna would officially be known around the world as the Queen of Pop.

Either unaware that disco was out or just too late to the party, Queen released their album Hot Spice to critical and commercial failure. The disco/pop-influenced atrocity nearly decimated the band's reputation in one fell swoop. Their standing as rock gods in Britain wouldn't be repaired until 1985, when Freddy Mercury gave the performance of his life on the stage at Wembley during the Live Aid concert. In the States, it would affect their sales until his untimely death in 1991.

Steven Spielberg's E.T. the Extra-Terrestrial was the biggest hit at the cinema, raking in nearly 800 million, and it cemented the director as the biggest hit-maker of our time. Spielberg had come up with the idea when remembering an imaginary childhood friend he had created during his parent's divorce. Much like George Lucas's Star Wars, E.T. would not only clean up at the box office but in the merchandise market too. Many movies such as Mac and Me would try to replicate its core idea and success, with none of them coming even close.

Smashing all previous box office records, including that of the aforementioned Star Wars, E.T.'s performance wouldn't be beaten for 11 years when another Spielberg-directed movie, Jurassic Park, was released in 1991. Other films to do well that year included An Officer and a Gentleman starring Richard Gere in his iconic role, the horror flick Poltergeist, and the third installment of the Rocky franchise.

In Britain, unemployment had risen to a staggering 3,000,000. The tensions in the streets rose even higher, and it seemed to most that the increase in joblessness would only ever grow. There was nothing being done for the public to think otherwise, and one riot or IRA bomb followed the next. Morale was at an all-time low, and Margaret Thatcher and her party faced new, ever-more heated questions every day.

With all of this going on, a small but very significant overseas war broke out on April 2, when Argentine forces invaded the British-claimed but lightly armed Falkland Islands. Most of the other countries in the world and their leaders presumed the British would just let the South American nation have it, as it had been an Argentine territory before the UK claimed it in 1833, but surprisingly—and despite the strains on the economy back home—Margaret Thatcher deployed a large and expensive task force to sail the 8,000 miles to a recently-declared war zone.

The Royal Navy reached the Falklands in early May, and their submarine, the HMS Conqueror, sank the Argentine cruiser, General Belgrano, killing 300 soldiers on board. The British had greatly underestimated Argentina, though, and they lost several warships in an attack from the air when Argentine planes hit them with missiles. It would take nearly three weeks for British soldiers to get their forces onto the island, and on June 11, the battle for the island's capital, Stanley, began. By June 14th, the weakened and poorly trained Argentine troops surrendered, and the territory became Britain's once more. Although the war was relatively short-lived, the memory of it would live long in the memories of both nations' people.

June and July were intense months for Buckingham Palace, but for two drastically different reasons. On June 22, 1982, Princess Diana and Prince Charles had their first child, with the birth of Prince William. Charles would emerge from the hospital after the 13-hour labour to a huge crowd of supporters and reporters, who took up the chant of, "Nice one Charlie, give us another one," to which the tired royal replied, "Bloody hell, give us a chance!" (Ezard, Perera, para 5.)

The second event happened on July 9, when Mike Fagan scaled the 14-foot wall outside Buckingham Palace, climbed a drainpipe, entered the palace, and wandered into the Queen's bedroom at around 7:15 a.m. Fagan had triggered two sensor alarms, but police had switched them off, believing they were just a mistake or an electrical fault. Rumours that the intruder sat on the Queen's bed and had tea and chatted with her until security arrived were quashed in 2012 when the man himself said in an interview that she left instantly and waited outside until the police showed up to arrest him.

Sports in America continued to grow in stature, importance, and profitability, and in football, Super Bowl XVI was one to remember. For the first time since Super Bowl III, the final was contested by two sides making their first-ever appearance in the showpiece event. The game was watched by a record 85 million people live on TV and is still one of the most-watched broadcasts in American television history. In a tightly fought contest at the Pontiac Silverdome, Michigan, the San Francisco 49ers overcame the Cincinnati Bengals by 26-21 to claim the title.

In baseball, the St. Louis Cardinals defeated the Milwaukee Brewers by four games to three, securing their first World Series since 1967. In South Korea, the maiden game in the KBO League—the first professional baseball competition in the country— took place. The people of Korea instantly fell in love with the sport, and the KBO League is still the most popular sports competition in the nation.

The 12th ever World Cup was held in Spain in the summer of '82, with 24 teams from around the globe taking part. Argentina, who were defending the title they'd won in 1978, had the enigmatic Diego Maradona performing in his first finals. The man-marking and often brutal treatment inflicted on him by the opposition's defenders was so severe that it would blight the competition as a whole. The Argentinian team would end up going out in the second group stage in a disappointing campaign.

Another extremely violent moment would be inflicted by West German goalkeeper Harald Schumacher when his disgusting challenge on French player Patrick Battiston left the latter with damaged vertebrae and the loss of several teeth. Battiston would later slip into a coma, and the German keeper would go on to finish the game without even a booking. FIFA would change a lot of rules that gave attacking players more protection following the events in Spain that summer.

Italy went on to beat West Germany in the final to lift the third World Cup in their history and first since 1938. With more TV coverage than ever before and the bright, enthusiastic, and flamboyant performances by some of the lesser-known footballing nations, the World Cup had never been more popular. Football as a whole was becoming a global phenomenon.

This was also the year that the world was introduced to the Compact Disc, and much like everything we associate with the eighties, CDs were sleek, shiny, and cutting edge. Now even listening to music needed to be done at a quicker pace, and people could just skip a song at the touch of a button. Of course, it was a long way from digital downloads and Spotify, but still, the music lovers of the world were very aware that something in the industry had permanently shifted.

The world also saw the beginning of the Lebanon War and Ozzy Osbourne biting the head off a bat, proving that anger and hatred were as prominent as ever. Movies and music were more violent, and hooliganism was rife across Britain. It would be easy to look back on the eighties and dismiss it as an unsettling time, but that would be far from the truth. Barriers were still being broken down, and with channels like MTV and more and more advertisements being aimed at the youth, there were clear signs that the younger generation was starting to have a greater say.

We have to remember the bright colours of the eighties, the outrageous clothes, experimental music, and groundbreaking movies. It was a period when every new toy was so mind-blowing it became a must-have, and somehow, through all the atrocities, it was a decade of immense hope. People dreamed of making it to the top, and for the first time in history, such opportunities were afforded to everyone if they wanted them enough.

1983: Tom Cruise, Eddie Murphy, and Even More Unemployment

The Cold War continued to drag on when President Ronald Reagan sent 5,000 marines to Grenada after the government there had been overthrown in a bloody coup by soldiers trained in Communist Cuba. With tensions already at breaking point between the two nations, the attack could have easily sparked much more resistance than it eventually did. Reagan insisted that the invasion was a must, citing the fact that there were around 1,000 American medical students living there at the time. This was true, of course, but it was generally known that the primary reason was to disrupt the spread of Communism throughout the Caribbean nations.

In the same year, Ronald Reagan announced the new Strategic Defense Initiative in March. During the televised announcement, the U.S. President spoke of weapons and defense systems far beyond the technology of the time, leading some reporters to deem this fantasy program "Star Wars." As much as it seemed to some of the American public as another glorious step ahead of the rest of the world's nations, the advances promised were fantastical at best, and even though production actually did begin the following year, it was shut down soon after when funding ceased in light of the Cold War ending. No weapons were ever completed.

In Japan, computer game creation wizards and trailblazers Shigeru Miyamoto and Gunpei Yokoi revealed their newest creation to the local arcades, Mario Bros. The platform-style game with increasingly harder and always colourful levels was actually a bit of a flop originally. The video game industry was in the middle of a huge crash, and the general appeal had worn off as advances were too slow to hold the attention of the youth. Miyamoto and Yokoi would not be deterred, though, and Mario and his brother Luigi would have to wait until 1985— when the home entertainment console, the Nintendo Entertainment System (NES), was released —to find the success we know them for today. Other games created by Shigeru Miyamoto through the years include The Legend of Zelda and Donkey Kong.

Also on the technology front, the first commercially produced mobile cell phones hit the market, with the Motorola DynaTAC getting FCC approval in the US in September of '83. Although something that would be considered a brick in our iPhone and Samsung world, it was seen as something of a technological miracle at the time. Taking 10 hours to charge in exchange for 30 minutes of talk-time and costing a whopping $3,995 (almost 10 grand today after inflation), the chunky Motorola was only realistically available to the very wealthy.

American television saw a monumental first and last. The timeless children's TV show Fraggle Rock had its maiden airing in January of '83. It was one of HBO's first original shows and was the creation of the now-legendary Jim Henson. His Muppets would entertain kids of all ages for years to come, and in 2022, a reboot aired on one of the world's biggest streaming sites. A show that was based around peace and love for all, it would be aired in over 100 different countries in its zenith.

The much-loved and long-running CBS series M*A*S*H came to an end in the same year, and an almost unfathomable 125 million Americans tuned in to say farewell to their favourite characters. The wartime comedy-drama show paved the way for the slightly deeper sitcom than those that had come before, and aspects like character growth and sentimental moments were groundbreaking in the TV show comedy world. Having run from 1972, the series produced 256 episodes and many, many moments that will forever remain on top 10 lists worldwide.

At the box office, the third installment of the Star Wars trilogy crushed everything in its path - as everyone knew it would. Raking in just under 500 million worldwide, it confirmed that the eighties was indeed the decade of the blockbuster. Eddie Murphy, fresh off the success of his Hollywood debut in 48 Hours the previous year, wowed audiences once more with his enigmatic performance in Trading Places. Although Dan Aykroyd was officially the star, Murphy stole the show, and he would go on to be one of the most bankable performers of the eighties and nineties.

Another star to break out into future astronomical fame that same year was Tom Cruise, whose role in the teen comedy Risky Business shot him into the stratosphere. The scene of him dancing in his socks and underwear as he slides across the polished floor is still parodied today, and Cruise would soon be the poster boy of everything that eighties cinema and being a celebrity represented.

In music, David Bowie's latest morphing act into a more pop-like, dance-based style worked a treat, and his 15th studio album Let's Dance would go on to be his biggest-selling record up to that point. Bowie, who had usually steered clear of anything mainstream, still managed to take a genre that had been threatening to go stale and breathe new life into it. This was all just another testament to the genius of the man. Bowie would also continue his foray into acting that year with the release of the cult classic, The Hunger, starring alongside Hollywood alumni Susan Sarandon.

Irish rockers U2 continued their unexpected rise when their third studio album War debuted at number one in Britain. Of course, the band would soon be huge in the States too, and they were one of several guitar-based bands that refused to be sucked into the more synth-styled groups of the time. Other rock bands were forming too, and American rockers Metallica released their debut album Kill 'Em All, which is still recognised today as the birth of thrash metal.

In Britain, unemployment continued to rise, and in 1983, it was recorded to be at its highest number since the Depression in the 30s, having grown to a terrifying 3,000,000. With this came even more riots, and it seemed like something could kick off on every street corner at any given time. Despite this, Britain continued to stand tall, and the inherent battling spirit of the whole nation that was causing them to lash out would ironically be the very thing that would get them through it all in the end.

With the horrors of the Yorkshire Ripper still fresh in the memories of the British public, the nation was rocked again with the arrest of Dennis Nilsen in February. After a plumber had been called to his shared residence on Cranley Gardens because of clogged drains, the worker discovered small bones that looked strange to him that were causing the blockage. After checking more closely, he suspected that they might actually be human remains, so he contacted the police who arrived on the scene.

It would soon be discovered that Nilson had murdered, mutilated, and dissected the bodies of many young men, which he then flushed down the toilet over long periods. Nilson admitted to the murders not long after his arrest, and the public would be horrified all over again as the gruesome details emerged in the press. The total number of victims will probably never be known, but it is suspected to be anywhere between 12 and 15. Nilson had been able to go undetected for so long because he targeted drifters and runaways, making it harder for police to know when someone had gone missing. He showed no remorse for his horrendous crimes.

In September, the Maze Prison escape in County Antrim, Northern Ireland, baffled not only Britain but the world. Maze was considered to be the most secure prison in Europe, yet somehow 38 IRA prisoners managed to pull off the greatest escape in British history in a violent break that sent shockwaves through the British prison system. Using guns and knives that had been smuggled in over time, and building friendships with several of the prison officers through the years in a carefully executed charm offensive, the 38 escapees managed to force their way out by commandeering a food delivery truck and overpowering several of the prison officers. One of the guards caught up in the melee was stabbed three times and would die of a heart attack soon after. Only 16 of the IRA members would be caught again after the escape.

In the British footballing world, Liverpool legend Bob Paisley announced that the 82/83 season would be his last in charge of Liverpool. A young Kevin Keegan joined Newcastle United from Southampton for £100,000 (approximately $130,000 US), and a 37-year-old George Best signed for Third Division Bournemouth. Ipswich Town manager Bobby Robson also left in the summer to take the England job two days after the country's poor showing at the '82 World Cup. He would remain in the role for eight years.

Bob Paisley would go out on the perfect high, guiding Liverpool to their third successive league title and the League Cup. The English domination of European competition came to an abrupt end, though, with only Aston Villa winning the Super Cup with an impressive 3-0 victory over the mighty Barcelona. In the FA Cup, Ron Atkinson continued his revamp of Manchester United by beating Brighton by four goals to nil in the end-of-season showpiece at Wembley stadium.

It seemed that 1983 was a time for technical advances, and the resurgence of the video game was on the periphery of climbing to unforeseen levels. Not only would arcade games see a massive rise in popularity, but the home entertainment console was being thought up behind closed doors, gearing up to take the world's kids by storm. Music was being digitised, and the special effects people were seeing in movies like Star Wars were like nothing ever imagined.

Britain had been gut-punched by the horrors of another serial killer so soon after the capture of the

Yorkshire Ripper, and the IRA continued to strike fear into the public. Even amidst the racial tension, fighting in the streets and on the terraces, political unrest, and the growing unemployment, the lower classes realised that they had to come together to stand a chance. As has been the case throughout history, hard times were producing some of the world's greatest artists, and music, film, and literature had a new, sharper edge.

We may look back on some of the harsher moments of the eighties and wonder if the people who experienced the turbulent decade—especially in Britain and Ireland—felt down about it all. But if you ask the majority who actually lived it, they would tell you honestly that it was the greatest decade in history for them. That's what makes the human race special: we find the good in everything, and that was what 1983 was all about.

1984: Band Aid and Michael Jackson on Fire

Britain's economy and morale took yet another body blow—this one almost fatal—in March of 1984, when the National Union of Mineworkers (NUM), led by Arthur Scargill, went on strike amidst multiple planned coal mine closures across the land. The NUM faced stiff opposition from the National Coal Board—a government agency—and the Prime Minister, Margaret Thatcher. Seen by many today as one of the most drawn-out and devastating strikes in history, the announcement of all the country's mineworkers laying down their tools for the foreseeable future was met with severely split opinions.

It would all escalate to unimaginable heights in November when two miners protesting at the time dropped a massive cement paving stone from the Rhymney Bridge onto a passing taxi below. Inside the vehicle was a man named David Williams, a miner who had continued to work throughout the strike. He would escape with only a few scratches, but the driver, David Wilkie, died at the scene. The incident shocked the whole of Britain, and with the strike already having dragged on for six months at the time, it now seemed that any form of compromise had been blown even further apart.

By the time Christmas rolled around, almost half the coal miners in the country would remain out of work. With the government having cut off any unemployment benefits for those striking, the families of the men who refused to return to work struggled desperately. Each month, the news would break of small groups of a few hundred losing their will and returning to work under their original conditions, but enough held strong as to bring the British coaling system to a near-halt.

Also, in March, iconic stand-up comedian and English TV personality Tommy Cooper died on stage before thousands in attendance and millions of viewers when he collapsed in the middle of his live set on the London Weekend Variety TV show, Live From Her Majesty's. Cooper, known for his heavy drinking and chain-smoking, was pronounced dead at the hospital soon after, and reports of his death the following morning were met with nationwide sadness.

Even as he was being taken away in an ambulance, the broadcast continued, and the other acts that had been set to follow him had to do so on the very stage where he had just dropped dead moments before, in a move from producers to not lose out on viewership. Such an act was seen as despicable by most and was only surpassed when the video of the comedy legend falling backward on the stage was leaked on a major streaming site in 2009.

As the cold weather kicked in with little coal to burn, British hearts were warmed and their spirits lifted by the most unlikely of sources. At the Winter Olympics in Sarajevo, two people pretty much unknown to the general public before then caught the nation's imagination when they performed together in the figure skating category. On a Valentine's Day that would be remembered forever, Jayne Torvill and Christopher Dean emerged on the ice to the sound of Ravel's "Bolero" and produced one of the most memorable moments of any Olympics in history.

Over 24 million people back home in Britain remained glued to their television sets throughout the routine, and multi-millions more the world over watched on in awe. The ice-skating duo performed flawlessly, and as they fell to the ice in a flamboyant finale, everyone in attendance gave them a standing ovation. Three perfect 6.0 scores followed from the judges—a world record for any single performance at the time—and the pairing that would be now forever known simply as "Torvill and Dean" became unforeseen celebrities overnight.

In other sports, the Super Bowl showpiece of 1984 was amazingly overshadowed by the most unlikely of sources—an advertisement. Ridley Scott, who had directed the dystopian masterpiece Blade Runner a couple of years before, was the man behind Apple's Macintosh PC commercial that aired during halftime at Super Bowl XVIII. Styled on the George Orwell classic novel 1984, it was vastly original in its direction, with the average watcher still confused as to what the ad meant by the time it had finished. Of course, this brought unfathomable word-of-mouth promotion, and many tabloids, magazines, and news channels spoke of it for weeks after.

Ridley Scott had been given the idea by advertisement pioneers Steve Hayden, Brent Thomas, and Lee Clow. The starring role had gone to an uncredited and unmentioned Anya Major, an English athlete. Given the advertisement's large scope and outrageous concept, Scott was asked to work on a relatively small budget, forcing him to hire hundreds of local skinheads to play the pale, lifeless drones. Each of them was given $25 for their time, and the tagline "On January 24th, Apple Computers will introduce Macintosh. And you'll see why 1984 won't be like 1984!" was etched in the public's memory forever.

The Super Bowl final itself was a one-sided landslide, with the LA Raiders smashing the Washington Redskins 38-9 at the Tampa Stadium, Florida. It was the first time the event had been hosted in Tampa, and it wouldn't be played there again until Super Bowl XXXII.

In the NBA, the Boston Celtics mirrored the final of '69 in both their opposition and the final score, beating the LA Lakers 4-3 overall. It was another epic encounter in the back-and-forth between the two sides that were already becoming such a legendary rivalry. Although the Philadelphia 76ers had taken the championship the season before and the Detroit Pistons would do so at the end of the eighties, the Lakers and the Celtics would amazingly share the other eight NBA trophies between them in one single decade.

The 83/84 season was also noted for the overtaking of Wilt Chamberlain as the competition's all-time career leader in points by Kareem Abdul-Jabbar on April 5th. Like something out of a Hollywood movie, it was Kareem's skyhook shot that claimed the record at the Thomas & Mack Center in Las Vegas. He would go on to beat and set numerous records throughout his 20-season career and is still noted as one of the greatest basketball players of all time.

In Britain, Joe Fagan took the hot seat at Liverpool, entrusted with continuing the almost unimaginable success of the previous years. He slipped in seamlessly, and Liverpool completed an unbelievable treble by winning the domestic league, the League Cup, and the European Cup. The latter was achieved via a penalty shoot-out in Rome, with enigmatic Liverpool goalie Bruce Grobbelaar managing to put off Roma penalty taker Graziani by shaking his legs before the player's run-up. The gesture would be forever remembered among football supporters as Grobbelaar's "spaghetti legs," and the resulting penalty was sent far over the bar. Alan Kennedy stepped up next, sending the Roma keeper the wrong way and securing Liverpool's fourth European Cup in seven years.

In other news, British Prime Minister Margaret Thatcher and Chinese Premier Zhao Ziyang met in The Hall of People in Beijing. The purpose of this first? To settle disputes between the two nations that had been there since the First Opium War in 1839. At the meeting, it was agreed (under the condition of a 50-year continuation of its capitalist system) that Hong Kong would be returned to the Chinese by 1997. The group of islands and tiny peninsula had been given to Great Britain by China in 1898 for an agreed 99 years.

On September 15, Princess Diana and Prince Charles had their second child, when Prince Harry was born to the delight of the general public. His mother, who had always said she didn't want her kids to grow up privileged, would spend a lot of time with Harry and his older brother William at fast-food restaurants, the local park, and even waiting in line with everyone else at Disneyland. All of this only endured the Princess to the public even more over the years, as she cemented her place in the watching world's heart.

President Ronald Reagan, who had seen his ratings drop during the first year of his reign, managed to win the voters back over by steering America through the recession in '83. Now that the majority of the public was back on his side, it was seen as the perfect time to try and win his reelection, which he did in 1984. His main opponent, Walter Mondale, had seen off the other leading candidates in the Democratic presidential primaries the previous year, including Colorado senator Gary Hart and African-American activist Jesse Jackson. Going up against Reagan would be a step too far, though, and the President of the United States would remain the same for the foreseeable future.

Eddie Murphy continued his astounding rise to the top of Hollywood's leading men category with the massive success of Beverly Hills Cop. The movie would top the box office in 1984, and with no special effects and a relatively unknown cast alongside him, it only proved how bankable he was becoming. Second on the box office list was a movie written by and starring one of Eddie Murphy's Saturday Night Live alumni, Dan Aykroyd. The timeless flick Ghostbusters also starred another up-and-coming comedian of the SNL crew, Bill Murray. Other hits that year included Gremlins, Splash, and Police Academy, proving that comedy was well and truly dominant in '84.

In music, the year belonged to Michael Jackson, who was on fire both literally and figuratively. At the Grammys, the soon-to-be crowned King of Pop won a staggering eight awards—seven of them for his album, Thriller, and one for his recording of the ET audiobook. A month before the awards ceremony, Jackson would make worldwide news when his hair caught fire while filming a Pepsi commercial. The incident would be parodied in comedy shows and movies for years to come.

With the famine in Ethiopia escalating, Band Aid—a charity music group set up by Bob Geldof and Midge Ure—recorded and released the song, "Do They Know It's Christmas?" The single, featuring mainly British and Irish musicians and celebrities of the time, was released on December 3, with the aim to send all of the proceeds over to Ethiopia and ease the struggles of those who were starving to death. After huge publicity leading up to the release, it would become the quickest selling single in UK chart history, and by the time the year ended, over 3 million copies had been purchased in Britain and Ireland alone.

Geldof had hoped that the single would raise £70,000 (just over $90,000) at best, but amazingly it would bring in over £8 million ($10 million US) in a 12-month period. Band Aid would also influence many other charities. The likes of Comic Relief and the Live Aid concert the following year would never have happened without Band Aid's creation and dogged determination to help those less fortunate.

In Britain, the year was unfortunately dominated by the miners' strikes and the now ever-present football hooliganism and unemployment. Finding something to smile about could be found in the local cinemas and on television screens, of course, and

British TV was in the midst of a comedic golden age. As is always the case with hard times, humour seems to find a way to prevail and thrive somehow, and smiling in the face of adversity is always the solution. To this end, 1984 was no different.

1985: Live Aid and Miners' Strike Ends

In July, one of the biggest gatherings of musicians—and most widely broadcast musical events—in history happened when Bob Geldof and Midge Ure successfully pulled off the Live Aid concerts. The main gig at Wembley produced an endless number of monumental moments, none more so than the magnetic and powerful performance by Freddy Mercury and his band, Queen.

With over 1.9 billion people watching on TV in more than 150 countries, Queen took to the stage amidst the general feeling that their time had come and gone. Their 1982 album, Hot Spice, had been a monumental flop, and the unsuccessful foray into disco and pop was seen by many of their fans as a betrayal. Taking to the stage in front of a 72,000-strong crowd and the TV cameras, Mercury burst straight into the opening of Queen's massive hit, "Bohemian Rhapsody." That was all the crowd needed, and by the time their six-song set was over, the performance was etched in the history of music as one of the greatest there ever was.

Several other similar charity concerts took place worldwide, with the one at the JFK Stadium in Philadelphia the largest in terms of attendance. Other countries to hold Live Aid gigs were the Soviet Union, Australia, Japan, Yugoslavia, Canada, and

West Germany. Hundreds of acts and bands took to the many stages, with the likes of David Bowie, Status Quo, Paul McCartney, U2, The Who, Elton John, Black Sabbath, Run-D.M.C., Bryan Adams, The Beach Boys, Santana, Madonna, Eric Clapton, Mick Jagger, Led Zeppelin, and many, many more performing their biggest hits. Michael Jackson and Bruce Springsteen's absences were questioned and seen as selfish.

At the movies, only one release really mattered, and it was something that nearly never got off the ground. Written and directed by the up-and-coming director and Steven Spielberg-promoted Robert Zemeckis, Back to the Future was all anyone could talk about. Spawning two sequels, a cartoon spin-off, merchandise, and endless classic moments, the time-traveling epic stayed in the hearts and memories of everyone who saw it. It continues to wow audiences to this day, and for a lot of directors, it is the highest bar to aim for.

In America, one of the most famous advertising blunders in modern history occurred with the release of the soft drink New Coke. The Coca-Cola Company had been losing out in sales in recent years to diet sodas, non-cola flavored beverages, and Pepsi. The release of New Coke was seen as sacrilege among sugary drink lovers, and after terrible sales, the campaign was pulled after only three months. Coca-Cola would bring back the original recipe, rebranding it Classic Coke, while New Coke became Coke II.

Amazingly, the American public devoured the Classic brand once more, suddenly grateful that something they had taken for granted was back in their local 7-11 refrigerators. Some people still claim that the whole debacle was just a clever marketing campaign to publicise the original brand that had seen its sales drop. Coca-Cola has always denied this, but the entire thing is still used as a metaphor in the advertisement world as an if-it-ain't-broke-don't-fix-it warning.

Another American staple and one of the most iconic roads in history, Route 66, was officially removed from the United States Highway System on June 27, 1985. Having grown in popularity and prestige since its creation in 1926—and with massive help from the Bobby Troup song, "(Get Your Kicks On) Route 66" in 1946—the road was seen as the epitome of Americana—big, brash, and impressive. After it was branched into the Interstate Highway System, it seemed to lose some of its prestige, and it would soon be replaced on maps with the name Historic Route 66.

In basketball, the rivalry and domination of the NBA in the eighties by the Celtics and the Lakers took a back seat for a moment when a young Michael Jordan was named Rookie of the Year. Although still a long way from his head-spinning rise to the top, it was just another piece in the jigsaw that showed the eighties as the greatest era basketball has known.

But the fantastic pantomime that was the Lakers and Celtics continued when both teams reached the final. LA, who were being driven forward by an aging but still phenomenal Kareem Abdul-Jabbar and the ever-improving Magic Johnson, had finished the season with an impressive 62-20 record. Proving how close the teams were in quality, the Celtics had ended their campaign with a slightly better 63-19, giving them the home advantage in the final showdown.

It didn't pay off, though, and the Lakers ran out 4-2 winners to take home the title once more. The Celtics had been hoping to make it two in a row for the first time since their domination of the sixties but were pipped at the post by the Lakers. At the grand old age of 38, Abdul-Jabbar would finish the season by being the oldest player to that date to be named as Finals MVP, proving that age was just a number.

In England, Everton were the team to stop their city rivals, Liverpool, from notching up their fourth league title in a row. Building on their FA Cup success in the previous campaign, the lesser-known Liverpudlian club stepped out of their neighbour's shadow to win their first domestic league in 15 years. On top of that, they also grabbed their maiden European trophy in the form of the UEFA Cup Winners' Cup.

Sadly, everything on the pitch was overshadowed by two major disasters that year. The first happened in a Third Division match between Bradford City and Lincoln City on May 11th. The condition of the main stand at Valley Parade had long been criticised, with the old wooden structure outdated and a fire hazard. Piles of litter—mainly paper—had gathered in the crevice below it for years, and during the match, a man in the stand who had smoked a cigarette dropped it on the wooden floorboards and tried to put it out by grinding it under his boot. The butt slipped through the cracks and landed on the rubbish below.

At 3:44, as the teams prepared to come out for the second half, commentator John Helm spoke of a small fire in the main stand. With the high winds that day, the fire spread in under four minutes, engulfing the whole area. With many people trapped in their seats and with the ensuing panic taking hold, fans rushed toward the exit doors and turnstiles. They were all locked, and many were burned to death as they tried to force their way out. In the end, the blaze would take the lives of 56 spectators and injure 265 more.

Only 16 days later, in Heysel, Belgium, the European Cup final was overshadowed by another disaster, as Liverpool prepared to take on Italian side Juventus. Liverpool fans illegally passed a fence separating them from the opposition's supporters and continuously charged them. The stadium wasn't built for the extra weight in that stand, and in the commotion that followed, the retaining wall collapsed, killing 39 people and injuring hundreds more. It was another dark day in the world of British football hooliganism.

In a call that upset many Britons, it was announced by the government that a plan was in place to phase out the classic red phone boxes the nation was so famed for. Much like crumpets, tea, red buses, and pork pies, the red phone box was seen as a staple of Englishness, much like Route 66 is to America. In a year that saw Coca-Cola burned by their need to tamper with perfection, it seemed that the world's leading powers had learnt nothing from the New Coke debacle.

Something that would go on to be associated with all things English did begin in '85, though, with the airing of the first episode of the now-iconic EastEnders. On February 19, over 13 million people tuned in to watch the opening credits for the first time. The drama series, which was created by Julia Smith and Tony Holland, had already gripped the viewing public by promising intrigue, gossip, and scandal. With the rising sales of tabloid newspapers like The Sun and News of the World, it was no surprise that EastEnders was a hit. It offered the same sensationalised dross that was becoming so popular among the masses.

In the same month, 4,000 more miners returned to work, meaning under half the mining workers remained on strike. It was another chip at the resistance of Arthur Scargill and his National Union of Mineworkers. It all was proving to be too much for the resistance to take, and the nation was starting to wake up to the fact that going up against Margaret Thatcher and her government rarely ended well. It was either to stand with them or to be crushed.

It would all come to an end in March when the NUM caved, and the strikers returned to work en masse. It was a severe blow to the country's morale, as nothing had really changed, and the plans by the government and the National Coal Board to shut down many of the mines went ahead as planned, meaning all that really had been achieved for those who chose to strike was a year without pay.

The AIDS epidemic reached new heights in April when a British boy born in America where his father was working contracted the disease when given blood in an unnamed hospital in Washington, DC. Born with immune deficiency syndrome due to the transfusion, Anthony Thorpe would not live to see his second birthday. The news sent shockwaves throughout the world, and the shouts from the bigots that it was just a "gay disease" were finally being questioned and proven to be nonsense.

The IRA continued to strike fear into Britain and Ireland, and their mortar bomb attack on the Royal Ulster Constabulary (RUC) in February was another blow to Anglo-Irish relations. The blast, which killed 9 RUC officers and injured over 30 more in Newry, was the largest number of casualties suffered in one attack for the RUC. The British press deemed the day "Bloody Thursday," while Margaret Thatcher was just as scathing, rightly referring to it as a barbaric act.

An IRA member situated in Newry, Eamon Collins, was not involved in the attack, but he was arrested nonetheless and brought into police headquarters. After several days of intense questioning, he broke, turning into an RUC informant (or supergrass). His testimonies would lead to the arrest of dozens of IRA members and make him an outcast and a wanted man among his former terrorist colleagues.

The stadium disasters at Bradford and Heysel rocked Europe in a year of ups and downs. In the aftermath of the latter, the English FA and later UEFA would place a ban on all English clubs participating in European football for an unspecified amount of time. The miners' strikes had ended after a year, and unemployment stalled for a moment but didn't improve. But Live Aid sent millions of pounds to people in need in Africa, and Comic Relief was founded as a result, so even more good spawned from Geldof and Ure's creation. More concerts for charity took place around the globe, and even in the depths of their own despair, the British and Irish public—and much of the Western World—found the time to help those they considered less fortunate.
It was clear that in 1985, the indomitable spirit and selfless nature of the world were in full effect.

1986: Chernobyl and Hands Across America

After a slight halt in the unemployment growth in Britain the previous year, the numbers saw another frustrating spike in 1986, meaning that there had been over 3,000,000 Britons out of work for three years - something which hadn't happened since before World War I. It was getting harder and harder for the public to look forward, and a grey bleakness seemed to have fallen across the Home Nations.

Despite the obvious lack of strength in the British economy, plans to build the Channel Tunnel between England and France were announced in January. At a potential cost of £7 billion ($9 billion US), the grumbles that could be heard from those still out of work were palpable and understandably so. But as often happens in such times throughout history, national pride can trump such emotions, and the idea of being native to such an astonishing feat of creation was hard to resist.

The impressive undertaking was promised to be completed by 1993, with Margaret Thatcher and French President François Mitterrand signing off on the plans to dig 130 feet under the Channel bed. The double tracks would run for 30 miles between Dover and Calais, with an added motor tunnel suggested for completion by the end of the century. As impressive as it all sounded, it seemed that the funds might have been better used elsewhere, especially in Britain.

On April 26th, a flawed reactor design, untrained personnel, and terrible safety measures combined tragically when an explosion in a nuclear power plant in Chernobyl rocked the country and stunned the rest of the world. The nuclear disaster is still seen as the worst of its kind in history, and the 28 deaths in the first few weeks were far from all the damage caused. Over 5,000 people in the surrounding areas developed thyroid cancer from exposure to radiation in the aftermath—with at least 15 of them losing their lives—and more than 350,000 additional people were evacuated, essentially losing their homes.

Rumours of cover-ups and false numbers concerning casualties and the devastating after-effects still rage to this day, and many people and their children still suffer from what happened. A lot of it could be put down to the Cold War, with the Soviet Union being left behind in certain scientific advances and unwilling or unable to learn from their peers in other nations. Whatever the case may be, Chernobyl was a hard-earned lesson in the vital importance of safety measures, especially when dealing with something so powerful.

With the AIDS crisis growing all the time and the fear surrounding it increasing daily, the UK government allocated £20 million (the equivalent of

$26 million US) to an advertising campaign aimed at teaching people how to avoid contracting the disease and relieving some of the stigma attached. Even though HIV and AIDS had been around for years, the general public's education on the matter was shockingly backward. Still seen by many as something for the homosexual population to worry about, this sort of backward thinking wasn't helped when the always-dangerous Edwina Currie—who was staggeringly named Junior Health Minister in '86—told the nation not to worry, as good Christians don't get AIDS.

The woman who was having an affair with soon-to-be Prime Minister John Major at the time also commented on the coal shortage by saying that the older generation needed to stop whining and just wrap up warm in winter. She would have her own foray into politics later in life and release six best-selling novels, proving that controversy, scandal, and general mouthiness were all a person needed to rise to the top.

In a darkly ironic twist, the man who had previously steered Britain through an age of unemployment, and done so successfully, died at the age of 92. Harold Macmillan was beloved by the British public for his wit, war service, and for always following through on his promises. His death, four days after Christmas, was still a shock, even considering his age, and in a final farewell that was befitting of the man, his last wishes for a private funeral and not a big, expensive showpiece was the perfect send-off.

On a dark day for NASA in January, the space shuttle Challenger—on its tenth orbital mission—exploded 73 seconds after takeoff over Florida. Of the hundreds watching from the launch site, several were the family of 37-year-old Christa McAuliffe, a high school teacher who had won a competition to become the first regular U.S. citizen in history to go into space.

McAuliffe had undergone several months of heavy training in order to be appropriately prepared for the exertions of space travel, and the launch had also been delayed for just under a week due to terrible weather conditions. By the time NASA had cleared the shuttle for takeoff, the weather was still the worst on record for such an event, and the cold air was the reason for the rubber O-ring elasticity being affected, making them unable to seal the joints. All seven people on board were killed instantly.

The mission had been created for the other six crew members to deploy a communications satellite to study Halley's Comet more closely than ever while it was in orbit. The world's most famous comet—and the only one known to pass by twice in a person's lifetime—was and is an anomaly in itself, in that every time it passes by Earth, it is always visible to the naked eye. With a round-trip of 75-76 years, the next time we can all expect to see it is due to happen in 2061.

Following on from the world's coming together the year before with the Live Aid concerts, Hands Across

America—a public event organized to raise funds for poverty and homelessness—took place on May 25th, 1986. The idea to form a human chain linked by people's hands was the brainchild of Ken Kragen, a music and television producer who had been behind the previous year's charity single, "We Are the World." With most participants asked to donate $10 for their spot in the chain, an estimated $34 million was raised. Sadly, less than half of that went to those less fortunate as in typically American over-the-top style, the rest went on needless operating costs and gimmicks.

The 40th season in the NBA saw the pendulum shift back toward the Celtics once more as they continued their "you're it" back-and-forth with the Lakers. Although the final didn't feature their great rivals of the eighties, the Celtics were still tested, running out eventual winners by four games to two against the Houston Rockets. Larry Bird continued his impressive growth as one of the all-time greats by grabbing the Finals MVP award.

With no European football to play following the Liverpool fans' poor showing and resulting disaster at Heysel the previous summer, English supporters still didn't seem to get the hint. Hooliganism was not only rifer than ever by '86, but it was now becoming fashionable, with most teams having organised and more professional 'firms.' Now referring to themselves as 'casuals,' these groups were renowned for wearing top-of-range clothes, such as Fila, Stone

Island, Lacoste, and Adidas, making it harder for police to differentiate between rival groups now that they weren't wearing their local side's colours.

The government continued to crack down on the hooligans, though, constantly bringing in stricter laws and quicker sentences. It didn't seem to make any difference, and in August, the rival firms of Manchester United and West Ham clashed on a SeaLink ferry, causing severe damage and many injuries. Eight of the culprits were arrested, with unprecedented lengthy sentences handed down to each of them.

That summer saw one of the greatest World Cups of all time take place in Mexico. In an event that would throw up seemingly endless cherished moments, the two most remembered not only came in the same game but from the same player. The first, now dubbed the "Hand of God" by Maradona himself, saw him become an instant villain among English supporters when he scored the opening goal of the match with his hand. The goal stood, and as Maradona ran away in celebration, the millions watching seemed to be only waiting for the referee to disallow it.

As the game progressed, the English defense tried to get closer to the mercurial Argentinian, who was widely considered the best player in the world at the time. Their efforts proved fruitless, and following his horrendous treatment at the previous tournament and the new rules protecting skillful players because of it, Diego Maradona caused havoc on the pitches of Mexico once freed of his shackles.

His second goal was a polar opposite of his Hand of God effort earlier, as he picked the ball up in his own half and spun his marker. Taking off at full speed, he managed to weave his way through what seemed like the entire English defense, shimmying his way into the box before rounding Peter Shilton and slotting the ball into an empty net. The goal is rightly known as the greatest ever scored in a World Cup, and given its importance and the stage it was scored on, many would argue that it is the greatest of all time in any event in football.

The announcement of the Channel Tunnel meant that two countries separated by an ocean would soon be connected. It would be a wondrous feat once complete and a testament to the power that the human race could produce when working side by side, or hand in hand, as was proven when millions of people linked themselves together across the States.

1987: Unemployment Finally Drops

In something thus far unachievable in Margaret Thatcher's reign, the unemployment rate dropped, going below the 3 million mark for the first time since 1981. Despite the nation's struggles in the previous years, 1987 also saw the Prime Minister reelected for a third stint with yet another landslide. It was a testament to her determination and the trust still afforded her that despite the lack of jobs, miners' strikes, and the constant threat of the IRA that the public continued in their seemingly unshakable loyalty.

A lot of this had to do with the results that were starting to be seen and Mrs. Thatcher's stricter policies and promises. Although the previously mentioned problems were still there, the PM constantly brought in stricter laws and harsher sentences to combat them. The clampdowns now covered a wide variety of criminal behavior, and it seemed like daily warnings were being aimed at the IRA, the rioters, and the hooligans in the football stands.

One such event happened early on the morning of January 20th, when police made several raids on the homes of the most notorious firms in British football. Operation Fulltime had been in progress behind the scenes for over five months as police gathered information on the main hooligans' whereabouts and activities. At six in the morning across London, the Midlands, and the Home Counties, both uniformed and non-uniformed cops arrived at the doors of several firms' "top boys," waving arrest warrants and taking the sleepy men into custody.

Through the successful raids, police found knives, air rifles, machetes, and even a spiked ball and chain. By the end of the day, 26 arrests were made in what was, up until that date, the largest scale sting in football hooligan history.

In keeping with the crackdowns, a joint Special Air Service (SAS) and RUC operation to ambush IRA members started and ended in the village of Loughgall, Northern Ireland, on May 8th. The ambush, set up after the SAS received insider information that the IRA would be hitting the RUC base that day, went successfully in so much as the eight-man terrorist group were all killed. It was the largest single death toll for the IRA in one go since the start of the Troubles.

It didn't deter the IRA, though, and in October, they detonated a bomb near the Enniskillen war memorial during the annual Remembrance Sunday event. The ceremony, which was held every year to celebrate British war heroes, was attended by hundreds of civilians. After the explosion, the terrorist group tried to claim that their targets had been the British soldiers attending the parade, but instead, they ended up killing 11 innocent people and injuring 63 more.

Several of those who died and many more severely injured were elderly, and the attack is seen as a turning point in the Troubles. Now, even the most staunch IRA supporter on the streets was questioning their reign of terror. When the Loyalist paramilitaries responded in kind, bombing Catholic civilians, it seemed that things were on the verge of spinning out of control. The actions of both sides were widely condemned, and new, much more determined efforts were made to bring an end to the horror.

The whole of Britain and the world was left stunned and in mourning when for no apparent reason, 27-year-old Michael Ryan went on a six-hour killing spree in the quiet market town of Hungerford. Armed with several automatic weapons, Ryan spent the time randomly shooting at anyone who crossed his path, even his own mother. His motive and state of mind would never be fully understood, and at the end of the bloody massacre, he would take the coward's way out and put a bullet in his own head.

In the aftermath, the British government reacted in a way that their cousins across the pond could learn a thing or two from when they changed the laws concerning gun ownership within months of the tragedy. Even though Michael Ryan had acquired a lot of his arsenal illegally, the Firearms (Amendment) Act of 1988 severely tightened control on the possession of firearms and the criteria needed to acquire them.

After years of debate and testing, Michael Eisner, the then CEO of The Walt Disney Company, signed a deal with the French government to build a theme park in Chessy, France, a town just south of Paris. It would be called Euro Disney, and construction would begin the following year with hopes of being opened to the public in the early nineties. Many other countries across Europe were considered, including England, Germany, and Spain, but France won out—or lost out, in the opinion of many—in the end.

The NBA was rocked when the Boston Celtics' top draft pick, Len Bias, died of a cocaine overdose only two days after signing. It came at a time when several other basketball stars had been banned for drug and alcohol abuse, and it was all a rare stain on an otherwise unmatched decade in the sport.

The Celtics still reached the final, coming up against their bitter rivals from LA once more. The Lakers took the title back home—their fourth that decade—when they defeated Boston 4-2 after a pulsating six matches. Magic Johnson, who was now the league's star player, proved his worth yet again when he was awarded the Finals MVP in a season that also saw the star, one Michael Jordan, continuing to rise in the backdrop of the Lakers/Celtics rivalry. 73

Super Bowl XXI saw the New York Giants prevail over the Denver Broncos at the Rose Bowl to claim their first title in over 30 years. With the sport's popularity growing to unimaginable heights, the showpiece final was drenched in everything so wonderfully American. The Beach Boys, Neil Diamond, and George Burns were all part of the entertainment, and if companies wanted to get their advertisements on the TV in between the action, they had to fork out a cool $600,000 for 30 seconds of airtime.

The British invasion of Barcelona Football Club continued with the £2.8 million ($3.6 million US) transfer of Gary Lineker from Everton after only one season on Merseyside. The Catalan's manager was fellow Englishman Terry Venables, and Lineker would be going there to link up with former Manchester United striker and Welshman Mark Hughes.

Also on the move abroad would be another man from Wales—Liverpool's Ian Rush—who signed for Italian side Juventus for a record £3.2 million ($4.1 million US). As part of the deal, the lanky forward would be loaned back to Liverpool for an entire season before making the move permanent. After a relatively unsuccessful stint in Italy, Rush would return to Liverpool after only one campaign, stating homesickness and the Italian style of play as the reasons for his poor showing. His quote that living in Turin was "like playing in a whole other country" has been claimed as fiction by the man himself in the years that followed.

Rush's last season in his first spell at Liverpool would end trophyless, something that the Merseyside club wasn't used to in the eighties. London club Tottenham Hotspur had started to emerge as a force to be reckoned with, putting up a challenge for all three domestic trophies right up until the end. But in typical Spurs style, they choked, ending up with nothing but desperate claims that they played the best football to keep their supporters warm.

Everton—sans Gary Lineker—still won the league, while George Graham's first season as Arsenal manager saw them lift the League Cup. Coventry City won their first-ever piece of silverware, taking out Spurs 3-2 in the final at Wembley, and therefore compounding the poor North London club to the reality of having blown the whole season.

At the box office, comedy still appeared to be the order of the day. The classically eighties movie Three Men and a Baby topped the charts, and the equally forgettable Moonstruck was also near the summit. Some more substantial comedies were also released, including Good Morning Vietnam, Beverly Hills Cop II, and the first of the Lethal Weapon series. Amazingly, the best movie of the year didn't break the box office top 10, with Stanley Kubrick's wartime masterpiece Full Metal Jacket apparently a little too gritty for the soft-edged eighties in America.

In music, Irish band U2 continued to crack America, with their album The Joshua Tree reaching number one on the American albums chart. Two of its singles would also get the top spot on the Billboard Hot 100 charts, and their Beatles-inspired performance on a rooftop in LA brought even more attention.

The year also saw the release of Michael Jackson's Bad, and the five number-one singles it produced is still a record that is yet to be broken. Another former pop star who had decided to go it alone, George Michael, released his maiden solo album Faith in October of '86. It would be a major success, winning a Grammy for best album and selling over 11 million copies in the US alone.

American music—and music as a whole—had lost a lot of its edge as the eighties rolled on. Now, the gritty punk anarchy of the seventies was being completely replaced by keyboards and electronic sounds, and the pop stars who were being groomed were pretty and clean-cut, at least on the surface. From the outside looking in, the music and entertainment industry looked superficial at best, and the heavy makeup being worn by those representing it was only papering over the cracks of the sugary tunes being released. Style over substance was certainly the way things seemed to be moving.

With unemployment down to 2.7 million by the end of the year and several of the nation's more violent football hooligans behind bars, Britain seemed like it might just be on the up again. Even with the back-and-forth bombings between the IRA and the Loyalists, the former were starting to show cracks in their attempts at bringing the country to its knees. Was the faith shown in Margaret Thatcher by the British public starting to pay dividends? There was a long way to go, but at least now, there seemed to be some light at the end of the tunnel.

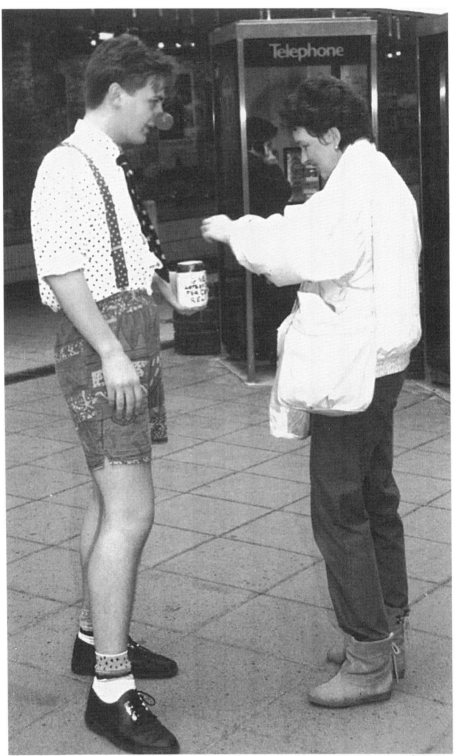

1988: Charitable Spirit of the Eighties

In early January, Margaret Thatcher became the longest-serving Prime Minister since the 19th century, when she clocked up eight years and 24 days in power. For most, it came as a surprise, as her tenure had started under such strenuous circumstances, given the state of the nation at the time. But the Iron Lady had proved to be hard of will—as well as heart, according to some—and her stricter laws and tighter control of funds were seen by many as exactly what the country needed. In hindsight, views on her time as PM remain split.

In a decade of charity and awareness, the first Red Nose Day was held in Britain, with most of the proceeds going to help relieve the famine in Ethiopia. It was another part of the already popular Comic Relief, started three years before by screenwriter Richard Curtis and apparent-comedian Lenny Henry. Its aim was to educate the public on the world's issues as well as raise funds while also doing so in a less depressing way than its predecessors. Comic Relief and Red Nose Day are said to have raised over £1.4 billion ($1.8 billion US) as of 2020.

More charity events took place that year, with Nelson Mandela's 70th Birthday Tribute concert taking place in front of a packed Wembley stadium.

It was broadcast in more than 66 countries to an estimated 600 million people. Although it was a charity event, a lot of what it was about had more to do with raising awareness, especially concerning racism and apartheid. Most of the political aspects of the shows—and the messages of love and peace they represented—were cut out by Rupert Murdoch's FOX television network, proving yet again the man's severe lack of humanity.

Throughout America, Britain, Africa, and most of the world, the AIDS epidemic continued to spread and strike fear into the general public. For those who had the disease, they were almost ostracized by their friends and neighbours, due in most part to the lack of education on the matter and the fearmongering of the newspapers and TV stations, especially in Britain.

Despite the best efforts of those who understood it to spread the truth, rumours would be believed over scientific facts for years to come, and by 1988, it was reported that around 50,000 people could have contracted HIV in Britain alone. The same report suggested that by 1993, at least 17,000 of these cases would result in death. At a time when TV coverage, newspapers, and magazines were more accessible than ever, it was just a pity the majority of journalists, much like today, had no scruples whatsoever.

Proving this point, Edwina Currie, who had claimed a few years before that "good Christians couldn't contract AIDS," was at it again when she claimed that over 90% of eggs produced in Britain contained salmonella. The disease, which had gained news coverage in the mid-eighties, had been a source of fear for an already frightened public. Currie's uneducated and unfounded comments caused a severe drop in egg sales across Britain, costing several people their livelihood and businesses their sales. I'm sure Edwina didn't mind all that, as long as the fame-hungry fraud's notoriety was increased as a result.

NASA resumed service, as usual, following the Challenger disaster over two years before when they successfully launched the space shuttle Discovery. Seen as a make-or-break mission in the Space Shuttle program, it became known as the "Return to Flight" mission, as NASA and the U.S. government continued to face damning questions as to space travel's importance. To combat the bad press, NASA stacked the flight with only veterans of previous missions, adding to the romantic element the people loved and basically hoodwinking them to the astronomical costs in the process.

On the streets of America, a new drug was doing the rounds, known by its nickname, 'crack,' and it would soon be seen as one of the most destructive narcotics to hit the country. A derivative of the already rampant cocaine, it was much cheaper and a whole lot more dangerous. With cocaine being seen more as a luxury drug for pop singers, movie stars, and

Wall Street suits, crack spread like wildfire through the lower classes, becoming an epidemic almost instantly.

The tides of change continued in Britain with the announcement that the classic pound note would no longer be legal tender. With the elimination of the sixpence earlier in the decade, and the plan to remove British Telecom's red phone boxes, many Britons felt the nation might be losing its identity. For the most part, though, the rest were trying to embrace what they felt was the British Isles' long-awaited foray into the fast-paced modern world.

Tom Cruise surpassed Eddie Murphy as Hollywood's leading man and most bankable star in '88 when he finished the year with two movies in the top 10 at the box office. The first, Cocktail, had every young man in America suddenly dreaming of becoming a bartender in a leading New York hotspot, while the second, Rain Man, proved that Cruise wasn't just a pretty face. Although the latter would win plaudits and awards for the performance of Dustin Hoffman, Cruise's first dramatic role rightly brought him a lot of respect too.

Rain Man would take the top spot in profits, but the groundbreaking Who Framed Roger Rabbit came a close second. Lover of all things special effects and computer-aided imagery (CGI), Robert Zemeckis, fresh off the success of Back to the Future, wowed audiences once more with his perfect mix of aesthetic and script. Christopher Lloyd would co-star with Bob Hoskins, and Lloyd's terrifying depiction of the cartoon villain had many children—and quite a few adults—hiding behind their popcorn.

In football, the biggest upset in the FA Cup's long history occurred at Wembley when minnows Wimbledon defeated the mighty Liverpool. The Dons, who had only been a league team for 11 years, shocked Britain and the footballing world when little Lawrie Sanchez headed in the only goal of the game from a Dennis Wise freekick. The Wimbledon goalie Dave Beasant became a double record-holder at the final whistle, becoming the first keeper to save a penalty in an FA Cup final while also being the first in his position to captain an FA Cup-winning side.

In a season of footballing upsets, the League Cup was won by lowly Luton Town, who were making their first appearance in the League Cup final. They went on to beat strong favorites and holders Arsenal 3-2 in a pulsating game at Wembley. Liverpool won the league at a canter, going on a 29-game unbeaten run in the process. Their nearest rivals Manchester United, being managed by Alex Ferguson in his first full season at the club, finished a respectable second given their previous woes.

The 1988 NFL season saw the final year in the career of legendary coach Tom Landry, bringing to an end his astonishing 29-year spell in charge of the Dallas Cowboys, a record that still stands today. Landry's experimental approach brought about many of the plays, tactics, and formations that are taken for granted in American Football today, such as the 4-3 defense and the "flex defense." By the end of his impressive coaching career, he would have amassed two Super Bowl titles, 13 divisional titles, and five NFC titles.

The NBA saw the Lakers retain their title with a 4-3 win in the final against the Detroit Pistons. In a masterstroke by head coach Pat Riley the year before, when he promised the people of LA a repeat performance in the '88 season, his words caused every team facing them to overthink simple decisions and play angry. It worked, but the Pistons were a hungry, up-and-coming team themselves, and the final defeat would work as all the inspiration they needed to go one better the following year.

1989: Guildford Four Released

In the year that brought the eighties to a close, one of the most significant issues of the decade in Britain continued its upturn in fortune from the previous year, with unemployment figures now recorded at 2 million. It was the lowest it had been since '81, and it gave the public a real sense of hope as they geared up for the next decade. This new, more positive vibe would be influential in the music, and the currently exploding Madchester scene in the north was a reflection of the swaggering attitude that would carry Britain and Ireland through the nineties.

Ecstasy pills were all the rage, and smiley face T-shirts represented a new era of peace and love that was spreading through the youth. Bands like The Stone Roses, the Happy Mondays, and the new rave culture DJs were replacing the more drab and depressing Morrissey and the mind-numbing repetitiveness of the likes of Duran Duran. Baggy jeans and loose T-shirts were replacing tight-fitting, shiny, synthetic clothes, and Manchester was amazingly becoming the cool place to live.

Along with the improvement in unemployment, the hooliganism element of British culture had been getting tackled too. It was still very prominent, but compared to the late seventies and the majority of the eighties, it was a lot less prevalent. This was mainly due to higher security at games, the gradual removal of terraces to be replaced by seating, and the government's crackdown on those arrested for football-related crimes.

Still, on April 15th 1989, one of the biggest tragedies in football occurred in Sheffield, when an FA Cup match between Liverpool and Nottingham Forest turned sour. The police would later be reprimanded for the part they played—or lack of a part, essentially—in the Hillsborough disaster, but the constant squeezing in of Liverpool fans who came without tickets was always going to cause issues at some point.

The rift between police and Liverpool supporters would never really heal, with one blaming the other throughout the years that followed. All that mattered were those who lost their lives, and placing blame will always become secondary. As Liverpool and Forest's fans spilled onto the pitch, those trapped became caught in a crush, with hundreds being pushed up against the fences and gates. With panic spreading through the already terrified crowd, disaster struck, and 97 people lost their lives.

As the dust settled on Hillsborough, 14 Liverpool fans were in the process of receiving prison sentences in Belgium for their part in the Heysel disaster a couple of years before. Over 200 supporters had originally been extradited to face charges of manslaughter, with the leading 14 culprits being the only ones to be sent to prison after a lengthy trial. Between them, they would serve only three years in prison, making the lives of the Juventus fans who died seem quite insignificant, and the general feeling was that much harsher sentences should have been handed down.

Tensions in the British streets may have been cooling a little, but there was still plenty of anger in the air, none more so than at Risley prison, Warrington, Cheshire. The building, which had been described as barbaric, squalid, unacceptable, and appalling the year before by an inspector, was famed for its brutal treatment of prisoners and the horrid conditions they were forced to serve their time in.

By the late eighties, overcrowding could be added to the list of issues at Risley, and in May of 1989, 120 inmates of the D wing gathered in the yard for what was to be an attempted sit-down protest against the terrible conditions. Plans changed, though, when a similar protest in the B wing the day before ended with devastating brutality when the ironically named Minimum Use of Force Tactical Intervention (MUFTI) squad broke the protest up with excessive violence.

Undeterred, the inmates of the D wing took control of the landing inside the prison instead, covering the stairs with liquid soap to stop the MUFTI squad from getting up to them. After barricading themselves off with unhinged doors and tables, the prisoners found their way onto the roof of the prison. Once there, the TV coverage started to spread, and the protestors knew their voice might just be heard. After three days of negotiations, they agreed to come back down peacefully, but with agreed-upon conditions that the state of the prison would be brought up to scratch.

Princess Diana endeared herself further to the public when she opened Britain's first AIDS centre in London on July 25. Outside, in front of the watching world, she gave Jonathan Grimshaw, a man who had been HIV positive for five years, a firm handshake. Unlike a lot of celebrities whose publicists instruct them to be seen at charity events or holding a sick child, Diana's gesture was natural, unplanned, and completely heartfelt. More importantly, it wasn't a popularity gimmick and just a personal gesture from a wonderful human being.

In one of history's most egregious misuses of power, the Guildford Four had received multiple life sentences in 1975, after the horrific IRA bombings of pubs in Guildford and Woolich. The police, who were under immense pressure to arrest someone, forced Gerry Conlon and Paul Hill to confess to crimes they had nothing to do with after nearly a week of intensive, non-stop questioning at the station. Broken and scared, the two young men signed pre-written confessions, which would also indict several of their family and friends.

After 14 years in prison and endless pain and suffering, the Guildford Four were given a new court date and eventually their freedom in 1989. The false evidence used and that which was covered up, along with the torture the men had faced at the station in '75, would shock the world. If Margaret Thatcher had given in to the public's cries for the death penalty to be reintroduced for terrorists years before, all of those wrongly arrested might have been hanged before their innocence was proven.

In America, the Republican party retained power for the third term—the first time this had happened since 1948—but there was still a change in personnel at the top. George H.W. Bush replaced Ronald Reagan, who was ineligible for a third stint as president. It was a sign that despite the crime rate, drug problems, and everything else that was happening, the American public still felt like things could be worse, and they would have been correct.

A day later, on November 9th, the Berlin Wall finally came down. Erected in 1961, it had separated many families and friends on the western and eastern sides of Germany and Europe for decades. With political views vastly different on either side of the bricks, tensions remained the same for years. By the time the wall came down in 1989, Germany and the rest of Europe seemed ready to move on. It was a pivotal moment not only in German history but that of the world, and the images of the Berlin Wall crumbling are as amazing today as they were back then.

With this monumental moment came the relative end of Communism, and a meeting between George

Bush and Mikhail Gorbachev—known as the Malta Summit—would result in the announcement that the Cold War was effectively over. Although nothing was signed at that point, it was still the most positive step to end the conflict since the war began in 1947. There are many opinions on the actual length of the Cold War, but often, it is best to just figure it from '47 through to the final dissolution of the Soviet Union at the tail end of 1991.

In China, one of the nations trying to hold onto their Communist identity, the student protests in Tiananmen Square, Beijing, showed that the younger generation wasn't as onboard with this mentality as those in charge. Thousands of students gathered in the square as they demanded more political freedom and less oppression. At first, the authorities didn't act, with two different viewpoints among the government still undecided. On one side, they thought maybe the protestors had a point and giving them just a little of what they wanted couldn't hurt. But the hardliners, who wanted to show they couldn't be challenged—especially by a group of young upstarts—won out.

The resulting massacre is a dark spot in China's history. Although no exact number of those slaughtered by police and military will ever be known, it was registered at 200. Years later, newly-released documents written by Sir Alan Donald—the then British Ambassador to China—revealed that he figured it to be closer to 10,000. Whatever the case may be, it was a despicable use of force by the Chinese government.

In the NBA, the domination of the eighties by the LA Lakers and the Boston Celtics was irreparably disrupted by the team that would earn the nickname "The Bad Boys" for their aggressive and often arrogant approach to games. The Detroit Pistons had lost the final the previous year in a tense seven-game encounter with the Lakers, but the new team on the block had learned their lesson fast, and the return fixture in '89 was a landslide. The Pistons won it 4-0, and a disappointing end of the season for the Lakers was compounded when their legendary talisman, Kareem Abdul-Jabbar, finally retired at the age of 42.

Under the dark shadow cast by the Hillsborough disaster, football in England continued to be played. With Liverpool reeling from what had happened to their supporters, they struggled to maintain their push for the title. Under the lights at Anfield, Arsenal came to Liverpool on the final day of the season, knowing they needed to win by two clear goals to clinch the championship.

The Gunners weren't expected even to come close to getting a draw, never mind a win, but a Michael Thomas goal in the dying seconds confirmed a 2-0 for Arsenal, meaning they would take their first league title in 18 years by one single goal. With both teams finishing on the same points, the goal difference rule came into effect, and what was left was the closest ever finish to a league campaign, and mathematically, the closest any can ever be.

Football would never be the same after Hillsborough, and the deaths of so many in such a terrible way were unforgivable. One positive did come out of it all, though, and new rules insisting that every team must have all-seater stadiums in the coming years changed the landscape of football safety. Now, it was becoming more of a family-friendly sport, and with Sky TV's dawning purchase of the viewing rights soon to come early on in the nineties, English football as a whole was going to be a better, safer, and more profitable sport.

The fall of the Berlin Wall and the positive steps taken to end the Cold War for good seemed like the perfect way to end the decade. Although the eighties —especially in Britain—had started off in anger and unemployment, things were beginning to look up. Among it all, cinema had gone to a whole new level, and even though the music seemed tacky and a little forced, for the most part, it was still a sign of free expression and love.

By the time 1989 ended, the world was ready to greet the nineties with open arms. It wasn't a gesture made in relief that the eighties were over, but more so the belief that anything was possible. Technical advances had accelerated at an unprecedented rate, but now, instead of the new gadgets only being available to the extremely rich and James Bond, they were mass-produced for everyone. Nintendo and Sega were making Game Boys and consoles that every kid wanted, and a whole new generation of gamers was being created.

Like every decade in history, the eighties built upon the one that preceded it while doing the groundwork for the one to follow. Given the obstacles put in front of the 1980s, I think it is fair to say they did a pretty good job on both fronts.

Conclusion

As the eighties drew to a close, the world saw the long-awaited end to the Cold War finally seem like a reality, and it would officially end in 1991. The Berlin Wall crumbled, and the German people and others across Europe were finally reunited. It was all a wonderful way to close out a decade that had its fair share of sadness.

Of course, the highs of the eighties had been something amazing. The technology being made available to the general public was like nothing they had ever seen before, and suddenly the average kid on the street had a console that was powerful enough to bring arcade-quality video games into his bedroom.

Music may have been more pop-like, but it was still producing classics. Michael Jackson was in his zenith, Madonna was bursting onto the scene, U2 were taking America by storm, and a little band called Nirvana were starting up in Seattle. The latter would throw mud all over the pristine shiny white facade of the musicians who had danced their way through the eighties, and music would take another sharp turn in a whole other direction in the nineties.

Unemployment in Britain had finally started to drop as the decade came to a close, and with the nineties dawning, the football hooliganism that threatened to ruin the sport was almost completely stamped out. In America, Ronald Reagan had steered the country through the tail end of their conflict with the Soviet Union, and his replacement, George H.W. Bush would see it out.

People were looking forward to the next decade, and with the advancements and entertainment being produced, they had a right to be just a little bit excited for what the future held.

References

Burkitt, S. (2020, November 1). Unemployment in the 1980s: "It felt like a bereavement." WalesOnline. https://www.walesonline.co.uk/news/wales-news/unemployment-1980s-it-felt-like-19149970

Ezard, J., & Perera, S. (2012, June 22). From the archive, 22 June 1982: Champagne and cheers greet Prince William's birth. The Guardian. https://www.theguardian.com/theguardian/2012/jun/22/archive-1982-monarchy-prince-william-birth

Jessen, M. (2022, February 25). Revisit Prince Charles and Princess Diana's engagement 40 years ago: "Whatever in love means." PEOPLE.com. https://people.com/royals/princess-diana-prince-charles-engagement-40-years-ago/

Ray, M. (2019). Live Aid | History, date, bands, & facts. In Encyclopædia Britannica. https://www.britannica.com/event/Live-Aid

Printed in Great Britain
by Amazon

14421716R00056